THE ILIAD

Introduction

The *Iliad* is a poem with 15,000 lines. It is thought to have been composed by a Greek poet called Homer, around 700 BC. Very little is known about Homer – but he is said to have been blind. This poem would have been told, or sung, to people who could not read.

The *Iliad* is called an epic poem, because it tells us the story of famous heroes fighting battles – battles between the Greeks and the Trojans. The Trojan War began because Paris, a young Trojan, persuaded Helen, the wife of the Greek king Menelaus, to go back to Troy with him. When the Greeks sailed to Troy, to take her back, the Trojans refused to let her go. So they camped on the seashore, by the side of their ships, to fight for Helen.

Homer does not describe the whole of this long war! Instead, the *Iliad* describes a few days of fighting during the tenth year of the war, which resulted from a quarrel between two Greeks: Achilles and King Agamemnon, the brother of Menelaus.

The battles between the Greeks and the Trojans are watched by the gods on Mount Olympus, especially Zeus, the most powerful god of all. They become involved in the Trojan War by helping their favourites.

In the *Iliad,* Homer shows that it is not actions that are important, but how bravely they face suffering and death in battle.

It is thought that Homer also composed the *Odyssey*. This tells the story of one of the Greek leaders, Odysseus, and his return home after the Trojan War had ended.

Some of the characters in the Iliad

Gods and Goddesses

Aphrodite daughter of **Zeus**; mother of **Aeneas**; pro-Trojan
Apollo son of **Zeus**; pro-Trojan
Ares son of **Zeus**; pro-Trojan
Athene daughter of **Zeus**; pro-Greek
Hera wife of **Zeus**; pro-Greek
Poseidon younger brother of **Zeus**; pro-Greek
Zeus the most powerful of the gods; sympathy for both Greeks and
Trojans

Greeks

Achilles son of the goddess Thetis, who protected his body from harm
– except for his heel
Agamemnon leader of the expedition to Troy; elder brother of
Menelaus
Ajax a good defensive fighter with a shield as big as a tower
Diomedes a great leader and **Athene's** favourite
Helen daughter of **Zeus**. Leaves **Menelaus** to run away with **Paris** to
Troy.
Menelaus husband of **Helen**; brother of **Agamemnon**
Nestor the oldest chief fighting at Troy
Odysseus quick-thinking fighter; favourite of **Athene**
Patroclus dearest friend of **Achilles**

Trojans

Aeneas second-in-command to **Hector;** son of **Aphrodite**
Chryseis daughter of a priest of **Apollo;** captured for **Agamemnon**
Hector son of **Priam**; leader of Trojan army; younger brother of **Paris**
Pandarus a great archer
Paris son of **Priam**; brother to **Hector**; takes **Helen** to Troy
Polydamas a great leader
Priam son of Zeus; king of Troy

CHAPTER ONE

The Quarrel

When Paris persuaded the beautiful Helen to leave her husband, Menelaus, and return to Troy with him, the Greek armies sailed across the Aegean Sea to claim her back. But they did not know how to get into that high-walled city. And the Trojans rarely left Troy, although Hector, Paris' brother, would have attacked the Greek camps if his father had allowed it.

As the war dragged on, the Greeks raided other towns, close to Troy, in search of slaves. A young girl called Chryseis was captured and given to King Agamemnon, the brother of Menelaus. Chryseis' father came to claim her back, but Agamemnon sent him away, empty-handed. On his way home, the old man prayed to Apollo, begging him to punish the Greeks.

For nine days, the Greek soldiers fell ill with fever.

On the tenth day, the swift-footed Achilles called a meeting. 'My lord Agamemnon,' he said, 'let us ask our priest to tell us why Apollo is so angry with us that he has sent this sickness.'

As he spoke, Calchas, the priest, rose to his feet. 'I can tell you why,' he said. 'It is because Agamemnon has captured Chryseis. Her father is one of Apollo's priests. This sickness will not disappear until she is given back.'

Agamemnon stood up, his eyes blazing like fire. 'Prophet of evil!' he shouted. 'Why should I not keep that girl? I like her better than my wife.' Then he paused.

'However, I am willing to give her up because I do not want my men to die. But I must have another woman in her place.'

'Where on earth will we find another girl for you?' Achilles asked. 'Give Chryseis back and, if Zeus allows it, you shall have your reward of Troy itself.'

'You are right Achilles,' Agamemnon replied. 'But if Apollo is to rob me of Chyrseis, I shall take *your* woman. I am a king and you are only my prince. Do not forget that.'

Achilles was so angry that he put his hand to his sword. 'You greedy fool!' he cried. 'You think that because you are a king, you can have whatever you want! I carried out that raid, yet you want to take away my prize.' But grey-eyed Athene came down from the skies to cool his anger. She stood behind Achilles and held him back by his auburn hair.

Yet Achilles had the last word. As he got up to return to his own camp, he shouted, 'You have dishonoured me, Agamemnon. I shall no longer fight for you, not until my honour is restored! I swear to you that you will need me one day.'

Chryseis was returned to her father, and the sickness disappeared from the Greek camp. Agamemnon had bulls and goats brought to the shores of the sea as sacrifices to Apollo. Then he sent for the fair-cheeked Briseis, Achilles' prize.

Achilles stretched out his arms and prayed to his mother, Thetis. 'Agamemnon has dishonoured me!' he wept. 'Go to Zeus and beg him for a Trojan victory. Then Agamemnon will truly feel the loss of me and beg me to join the fighting once more.'

Thetis did as her son asked. She made Zeus promise to withhold a Greek victory until the honour of Achilles had

been satisfied. Zeus sent a dream to Agamemnon, telling him to prepare his army for battle.

When dawn broke, Agamemnon sought advice about his dream. He was not sure whether he could trust it or not. So he decided to put his army to the test by telling them that they could sail home. His soldiers made for the ships; but one of his leaders, Odysseus, did not go with them.

'It would be humiliating to return home without Helen,' he told Agamemnon. 'We have already waited for nine years. It is no wonder the men are restless. Remember the priest's prophecy. Troy shall be ours.'

'You can see how Zeus torments me,' Agamemnon replied. 'He entangles me in angry quarrels with Achilles. But you are right. Let us prepare ourselves for battle!'

The army roared their approval as loudly as the waves crashed on the seashore. Like flocks of birds gathering in the river meadows, the soldiers took up their positions. Athene, who wanted only victory for the Greeks, encouraged them to fight. They advanced across the plain like a fire burning across the land. The earth groaned beneath them, like the thunder Zeus sends when he is angry.

Iris, the messenger of the gods, took the grim news to the men of Troy. Led by the great Hector, they took up their battle position on a ridge overlooking the plain outside their city. Next to Hector stood his brother, Paris – the prince who had stolen Helen away – draped in a leopard's skin. The Trojans advanced with shrieks and cries, like cranes screeching from the skies. The Greeks moved forward in silence, a cloud of dust rising from their marching feet.

And at last, the armies faced each other in battle.

CHAPTER TWO

Death in the Dust

Paris stepped out from the Trojan ranks, calling for the Greeks to send their best man to fight him. Menelaus, as pleased as a lion coming across a deer, jumped from his chariot.

'Now I shall have my revenge!' he thought. 'I'll cut him to pieces!'

But Paris, pale and trembling, ran back to the Trojan ranks, like a man who has caught sight of a snake.

'You are a disgrace to us all, brother!' Hector called to him. 'You took Helen, but you cannot stand up to her husband!'

Paris was ashamed. 'You are right to taunt me, Hector,' he replied. 'I *shall* fight Menelaus for Helen - a fight to the death. If I am killed, Helen and all her jewels will be returned to Menelaus. If he dies, she will remain here with me.'

Menelaus agreed and sent for lambs to sacrifice to the gods

The golden-haired Helen was weaving a purple tapestry with the other women when Iris came to her in the shape of her sister-in-law. When she learned that Paris and Menelaus had agreed to fight, she was filled with longing for all that she had left behind: her husband, her child and her friends. Veiled and weeping, she went to the tower, where King Priam and the elders were looking down over the battle plain.

When sacrifices had been made on the plain, the Trojans drew lots to see who would throw the first spear. The name of Paris was drawn from the helmet! Priam, who could not bear to see his son fight, rode back to Troy.

Paris and Menelaus put on their armour, picked up their shields and swords, and took up their positions between the two armies. They glared at one another, and excitement ran through the ranks. Paris hurled his spear and hit Menelaus' shield. Then Menelaus' spear ripped through the side of Paris' tunic, and his sword shattered on his helmet. Menelaus hurled himself upon Paris, like a panther, and dragged him by the helmet strap towards the Greek lines. But Aphrodite snapped the strap, and surrounded Paris in a heavy mist. Menelaus, furious, threw the empty helmet amongst his men.

'Trojans, listen to me!' Agamemnon shouted. 'Menelaus has clearly won the fight. The victory is ours. Now give Helen back to us!'

But Aphrodite did not want Helen to return to Menelaus, and ordered her back to Paris.

'No,' Helen told her. 'He is no longer my lord. Now my place is with Menelaus.'

'I could easily turn the Greeks *and* the Trojans against you,' Aphrodite whispered. 'Then *you* might meet a cruel death.'

Helen, terrified by her words, did as the goddess demanded. But she taunted Paris for losing the fight. And out on the plain, Menelaus prowled like a wild beast, searching for his enemy.

And there might have been peace, but for Athene. She flew to Pandarus, the best Trojan archer.

'Have you the courage to send one of your arrows, like a fork of lightning, against Menelaus?' she asked. 'You will cover yourself in glory if you kill such a Greek leader.'

In this way, the fool was persuaded. His feathered arrow winged its way into the enemy lines. Guided by Athene, it hit the buckle of Menelaus' belt, grazing his flesh. The wounding of Menelaus roused the Greeks to fight again. They put on their armour for the greatest battle in all the years they had faced one another across the plain. The armies advanced and met with a clash of shields and spears. A great din rose from the plain and the earth soon ran with blood. As the day wore on, the Trojans fell back, while the Greeks pushed forward.

Soon, dead Trojans and Greeks stretched out beside each other, faces down in the dust.

CHAPTER THREE

A Greek Hero

As the battle raged, Diomedes fought more bravely than all the other Greeks. It was Athene who made him bold. She thrust him, on foot, into the very heart of the battle.

'Diomedes,' she said, 'you can go and fight. I have filled your heart with confidence. And I have given you the power to distinguish men from gods. Do not fight any god, except Aphrodite. I do not like her. If you see her, stab her with your spear.'

The Greeks pushed back the Trojans, killing six of their leaders. Diomedes stormed across the plain like a winter river in full flood.

But when Pandarus saw Diomedes charging towards him, he bent his curved bow. An arrow hit Diomedes in his right shoulder, piercing his armour and splattering the bronze with blood. But it did not kill him. Diomedes fell back by his chariot and begged his friend to pull the arrow from his shoulder. Then, like a lion, he leaped into battle again and killed eight Trojans in his fury.

Aeneas, the second in command to Hector, went in search of Pandarus. 'Pandarus,' he said. 'Where is your bow? Where are your arrows? Let them fly at Diomedes once more. He has already killed some of our best men.'

'I can see the hand of a god in this furious attack,' Pandarus replied. 'A god, wrapped in mist, must be standing by Diomedes. I drew blood from him and Menelaus, but still they are not dead.'

'This is no time to talk,' Aeneas said. 'They win as long as we do not fight. Come, get into my chariot. We shall soon reach Diomedes.'

As Diomedes saw the horses speeding towards him, he thought, 'I shall go and meet them on foot. And I shall not run away in terror.'

Pandarus, close to his enemy now, hurled his long spear, piercing Diomedes' shield and reaching his body-armour. 'This time, the glory belongs to me!' he boasted.

'You did not hurt me!' Diomedes shouted, hurling his own spear at Pandarus.

The spear came down on Pandarus' nose, shattered his teeth and cut off his tongue. He toppled from the chariot, dead. Aeneas, fearing the Greeks would take the body, guarded it well. Diomedes threw a large rock at Aeneas, and Aeneas would have died, if Aphrodite – his mother – had not wrapped him in her shimmering robes, and if Apollo had not lifted him from the battle. Then Diomedes remembered Athene's words.

'Aphrodite is a timid goddess,' he said to himself. 'I shall soon catch her.' After a long chase, he lunged at her with his spear and pierced her flesh where the palm joins the wrist. 'Be off with you!' he cried. 'Stop interfering in our battles!'

The battle went on, swaying this way and that across the plain. Hector almost forced the Greek armies back to their ships. Then, as the day wore on, the tide of battle changed, and Diomedes and Odysseus pushed the Trojans back towards Troy. Hector, exhausted, left his command to Aeneas and returned to Troy. He commanded his mother to offer sacrifices to Athene. Then he went to find Paris.

Paris was in his bedroom, Helen by his side. 'What do you think you are doing, brother?' Hector bellowed. 'Men are fighting all around you because of what *you* did nine years ago! Get back into action before Troy goes up in flames! My heart aches when I hear the shameful names your fellow Trojans call you.'

As Paris went to arm himself once more, Hector said farewell to his wife and baby son. Then, side-by-side, the brothers rushed through the gates of Troy, anxious to do battle. And the Trojan army greeted them like a sailing boat that has waited a long time for a favourable wind.

When the Trojans saw Hector and Paris, they rallied. Many Greeks died in the fighting and many were driven back to their ships. When Athene saw the slaughter, she decided to stop the fighting that day. As she swooped down from Olympus to Troy, Apollo – who wanted a Trojan victory – stopped her in mid-flight.

'I have a plan that will end this bloodshed for a time,' he told her.

CHAPTER FOUR

Return to Battle

Apollo went to Hector in the shape of his brother, Helenus. 'Your time to die has not yet come,' he told Hector. 'The gods have told me so. Challenge the Greeks to a hand to hand fight.'

Hector's heart beat faster when he heard these words and he rushed out onto the plain to speak to Agamemnon. 'Let the man who is willing to take me on step forward!' he shouted. 'If your man kills me, he must let the Trojans take my body home for burial. If I kill your man, as Zeus is my witness, I shall send his body back to you.'

The Greeks listened to him in silence. Nobody came forward. At last, Menelaus sprang to his feet, groaning in disgust. 'What does this mean?' he demanded. 'Is there not *one* Greek warrior willing to fight Hector? Well, may you all rot, you gutless cowards! I shall fight him myself. The gods above will decide who wins.'

With these words, he put on his armour. But Agamemnon seized him by the hand. 'There is no need to be so foolish, brother,' he said. 'Hector is by far the better fighter. Even Achilles would fear to face him.'

Then Nestor, the oldest of the Greek chiefs who were fighting, reproached the Greeks, until nine men volunteered and lots had to be drawn. Nestor drew out the name they all hoped for – that of Ajax. The Greeks, when they saw him ready for battle, were full of joy.

Even Hector's heart beat faster at the sight of Ajax's

great shield, which was made of seven ox hides. With taunts and loud cries, he threw his spear at Ajax. It penetrated six layers of that thick shield. Then Ajax threw. His spear penetrated Hector's shield and part of his breastplate, but it did no further damage. When they had each pulled out their spears, they fell upon each other like lions. Ajax's spear grazed Hector's neck. Then he hurled a huge rock at Hector, who fell, but jumped to his feet again.

As night fell, the fight had to end. Ajax and Hector exchanged gifts and parted, agreeing to fight for victory some other time. And sacrifices were made that evening to the gods in Olympus.

The next day, it was agreed that there would be no fighting that day and that each army should use the time to burn its dead. Inside Troy, within Priam's palace, peace talks were taking place. Priam suggested that Helen should be given back to Menelaus along with all the jewels that came with her. But Paris refused to give up Helen, although he agreed to hand back her jewels.

As they talked, the Greeks built a deep ditch around their camp, which no chariot could cross. And on the land side, they built a wall with gates and towers.

Now the armies prepared for their second day of battle. The gates of Troy were thrown open and Hector led out foot-soldiers and charioteers. They met the Greeks with a great clash of shields and spears. All through the morning they fought. The air was filled with the screams of the dying – and the earth ran with blood.

When the sun was high, Zeus flashed a streak of lightning at the feet of the Greek army. Terror filled them and the blood drained from their faces. The Trojans were able to put the Greeks to flight.

'Trojans!' Hector shouted. 'Zeus wants to grant us the victory! The Greeks are fools if they think their flimsy wall can stop us. And once we get to their ships, we shall set fire to them.'

The Trojans surged towards the ships. And they would have reached them, if Agamemnon had not rallied his army. Now the Greeks fought hard again. But still the Trojans, led by Hector, drove the Greeks back to their ditch. Hera felt such pity for them that she and Athene spoke to Zeus. He had already foreseen what would happen.

'At dawn tomorrow,' Zeus told them, 'much of the Greek army, including Patroclus, friend of Achilles, will be destroyed. For Hector will give the Greeks no rest until Achilles comes back into battle.'

Night was falling on the plains of Troy. 'Only darkness has prevented me from destroying all their ships,' Hector cried. 'Now go and gather firewood to light the fires. We shall spend the night out on the plain. We do not want the Greek ships trying to sail home under cover of darkness.'

His men cheered loudly. They lay all night on the plain while a thousand camp fires burned. Round each one sat fifty men – all waiting for dawn to shed her golden light.

And so the Trojans kept their watch that night.

The Greek leaders were filled with fear at the loss of so many men. 'Zeus is to blame for this,' Agamemnon wept. 'He promised that Troy would be ours. We should sail home.'

'My lord, what is wrong with you?' Diomedes asked. 'Do you really think we are cowards? If you want to leave, then leave. But I shall fight until I reach Troy.'

Nestor rose to his feet. 'We must post sentries along the wall,' he said. 'The Trojan fires so close are not a pleasant sight. You gave way to your pride, Agamemnon. You

should make an apology to Achilles.'

And Agamemnon agreed, offering many gifts, including the woman he had taken from him. But Achilles rejected his offer.

'I no longer have any desire to fight Hector,' he said. 'Tomorrow, I shall make sacrifices to the gods and sail home. I hate Agamemnon's gifts as much as I hate him.'

The strength of his words amazed them all. Even his friend, Ajax, could not persuade him to change his mind.

'Forget whether Achilles stays or goes,' Diomedes said. 'When dawn lights up the earth, *we* must just fight on.'

CHAPTER FIVE

Spies!

As the Greek leaders settled down to sleep, Agamemnon watched the fires burning across the Trojan plain. He decided to speak to Nestor. Menelaus, like his brother, was also awake, and they stopped to talk.

'We must have a plan of action if we are to avoid defeat,' Menelaus said. 'In all my years of fighting, I have never seen a man inflict so much damage in one day.'

Agamemnon agreed and they went to wake Nestor, who called a council of leaders.

'Is there a man brave enough to make his way secretly into the Trojan camp?' Nestor asked.

Diomedes volunteered at once, asking only to take Odysseus. The two men put on their armour and, carrying two-edged swords, set out through the dark night like a pair of lions.

Hector, too, asked for somebody to spy on the Greek camps. Dolon, a wealthy young Trojan, volunteered for the task – in return for the horses and chariot of Achilles. But Diomedes and Odysseus saw him coming and lay among the dead bodies until he passed by. Then they gave chase.

The terrified and weeping Dolon, hoping to save his own life, told them everything they wanted to know: that King Rhesus, a new ally, with the swiftest horses in the land had just arrived and was camped to the east. Diomedes cut off Dolon's head as he was speaking and hid his body among the reeds.

Odysseus and Diomedes pressed on to the Trojan camp, where the weary Rhesus and his warriors were sleeping. Athene filled Diomedes with fury. Whirling to the left and right, he slew them where they lay. Odysseus untied the horses and they rode back to their ships.

The next morning, the Greek army was filled with the new desire to fight. No longer did they want to sail home. When Agamemnon killed six Trojan leaders, Zeus kept Hector safe. As the Trojans retreated across the plain, Zeus sent Iris with a message for Hector.

'As long as you see Agamemnon mowing down the Trojan ranks, retreat to Troy,' she said. 'But encourage your men to carry on fighting. If Agamemnon is hit and takes to his chariot, Zeus will give you enough strength to force the Greeks back to their ships.'

Hector leaped from his chariot at once and ran among his men, a spear in each hand, rousing them to fight. So the Trojans turned and faced the Greeks. Although Agamemnon was wounded in the arm, he continued to fight, until the pain drove him to retreat.

'Their best man is gone!' Hector cried out. 'Zeus has given me the victory. Now drive your chariots straight at the Greeks and win a greater victory.'

With these words, Hector set the proud Trojans on the Greeks. He flung himself into the battle, like a winter storm coming from the mountains, and killed nine Greek leaders. But Diomedes and Odysseus stood firm. Diomedes' spear knocked Hector to the ground and he was saved only by his helmet. He sprang into his chariot, escaping dark death once more. Paris saw his chance and aimed his arrow at Diomedes, pinning his foot to the ground. But Diomedes pulled out the arrow and let him be driven back to his ship in his chariot.

Odysseus now stood ringed by Trojans as hunting jackals ring a deer. He fought on, flinging his enemies from him as a boar flings off the hounds – and killing five of them. Then an enemy spear pierced his breastplate and blood ran along his body. Pulling out the spear, he called out three times for help. Menelaus heard his cries and pulled Odysseus into his chariot, leaving Ajax to carry on the fight.

Ajax retreated slowly, much against his will, only too aware of the danger to the Greek ships. The proud Trojans went after him, stabbing at his shield with their spears.

So they fought on like blazing fire.

And all this time, Achilles watched this sad retreat from his ship. He sent his friend, Patroclus, to ask Nestor about those who had been wounded.

'Why is he asking?' Nestor said. 'Achilles is a great warrior, yet he shows no concern for his fellow Greeks.'

Nestor recounted long stories of his bravery when he was young, when he had fought with Patroclus' father. 'Have you forgotten what your father said?' he asked Patroclus. 'He said that, although Achilles was the stronger of you two, you are the older. *You* should give Achilles good advice. It is not too late.'

'What shall I say?' Patroclus asked.

'Ask him to give you his beautiful armour to wear in battle,' Nestor replied. 'That will strike fear into the Trojans. They may stop the fighting for a while and give our exhausted men some breathing space.'

Nestor's words went straight to Patroclus' heart and he rushed to speak to Achilles.

CHAPTER SIX

The Battle for the Ships

As Patroclus went to talk to Achilles, fighting broke out once more between the two armies. Polydamas, a daring Trojan leader, called to Hector, 'We cannot drive our chariots across the ditch, for there are sharp stakes all along the edge. Then there is the wall. The Greeks will attack us if we are trapped. We should attack the wall on foot.'

Hector agreed. They lined up their men in five battle ranks, led by Hector and Polydamas, Paris, Aeneas, Sarpedon and two more of Priam's sons. They closed up their ox hide shields to make a barrier and advanced towards the wall. On the brink of the ditch, Hector and Polydamas saw an eagle in the sky, carrying a bleeding snake. It dropped the writhing snake amongst the Trojans and flew off.

'I must speak my mind, Hector,' Polydamas said. 'That snake did not get home. Even if we break down the Greek wall, we shall not be able to get back to Troy.'

'Foolish words, Polydamas,' Hector replied. 'I do not trust this omen. But I trust Zeus. We must defend Troy. And if you refuse to fight, I shall kill you myself.'

Hector's words put new courage into his men and they thrust forward again, with blood-curdling cries. But still they failed to breach the wall. Like flakes of snow, the Greeks hurled stones down upon their enemy. So Zeus sent his Trojan son, Sarpedon, into the thick of the battle. With his bronze shield and two spears, he hurled himself at the

27

wall like a hungry mountain lion. The noise was terrible as shields and spears clashed. Greeks and Trojans now hacked at each other along the wall.

The battle was even until Zeus decided to favour Hector. He gave Hector enough strength to hurl a great stone to shatter the gate before him. 'Forward, Trojans!' he called. 'Set fire to the Greek ships!'

Nobody could have held Hector back as he leapt through the gate, his face as dark as nightfall, his armour and spears gleaming. As the Trojans swarmed behind him, across the wall and through the gates, the Greeks fled back to their ships.

Zeus turned his eyes away from the battle by the ships and left them to fight, certain that no other god would interfere. But his brother, Poseidon, was also watching, and he pitied the Greeks. He strode down the rocky mountain, ordering his chariot to take him to the Greek ships.

Then, unseen, he called out to Ajax. 'You can save the Greek army if you fight with your old courage. The wall is safe, except for the place where Hector rages. Stand fast there.' Then he rallied the others, who were dead on their feet and losing heart. 'We must not give up. We must attack for the sake of our honour!'

The Greeks rallied. The Trojans still pushed forward, shields together, like a boulder crashing down a mountain slope. But they met a line of Greek shields and retreated. Men charged at each other like rough winds in a storm.

Ajax moved out to challenge Hector. 'Do you really think that you are going to destroy our ships?' he taunted. 'Soon Troy will fall to us.'

'What rubbish you speak!' Hector called back. 'You'll die with the rest of them. My spear shall cut you to pieces.' He led his men forward with a mighty roar, hurling his spear at Ajax. It missed his skin, settling on his shoulder straps. Ajax picked up a boulder and hit Hector on the chest, making him stagger. His second spear fell from his hand as he crumpled in the dust. The Greeks rushed towards him, crying in triumph.

The best Trojans, including Aeneas and Polydamas, protected Hector with their shields. Then they carried him back to Troy. Now, with renewed effort, the Greeks pushed the Trojans back through the wall across the plain.

Zeus woke up to see the Trojans being chased by the Greeks, and Hector coughing up blood. He was furious. 'This is my brother Poseidon's fault,' he said to himself. 'I shall tell him to stop this fighting at once.'

Poseidon was angry, too. 'What has this got to do with Zeus?' he thought. 'When the world was divided into three parts, I received the sea, Zeus the skies and our brother, Hades, the underworld. But the earth belongs to us all. I shall *not* do as he tells me. He can't scare me with his threats!'

Zeus called Apollo to help him, telling him to put new strength into Hector. Like a horse breaking from its stable, Hector ran forward once more, urging on his men. At first, the Greeks held hard, like a cliff of granite. But Hector attacked like a pitiless lion attacks a herd of cattle. Breaking the Greek ranks, the Trojans picked off their leaders, one by one. Diomedes, Odysseus and Agamemnon, all injured, retreated to Nestor's side.

Suddenly, the Greeks turned and ran.

'Hold your ground!' Nestor shouted.

'Defend the ships!' Ajax called. 'Fight like men!'

But the slaughter by the ships was terrible to see.

CHAPTER SEVEN

The Death of Patroclus

As the battle raged, Patroclus came weeping to Achilles.

'Friend, why are you crying like a young girl?' Achilles asked him.

'We are in terrible trouble,' Patroclus replied. 'All our best men are wounded or fighting by their ships. You and your pride! It is your fault! You have done nothing to prevent this destruction. Give me your armour. If the Trojans think you are fighting again, they will break off the battle for a while. I might be able to drive them away from our ships.'

Achilles, still speaking bitter words about his quarrel with Agamemnon, agreed.

'Yes, you must defend the ships, Patroclus,' he said. 'But do not fight too long. Do not lead your men on to Troy. Turn back when you have saved the ships and leave others to carry on the fighting.'

Patroclus put on his friend's armour. Horses were fastened to his chariot. Then he rode with Achilles' men towards the ships. They swarmed like wasps around the Trojans, filling them with panic. Patroclus hurled his spear and killed their finest leader. The Trojans fell back with a great roar and the Greeks poured forward. Each one killed a Trojan leader, including Sarpedon, the son of Zeus.

As the Trojans retreated, Patroclus chased after them, filled with revenge. He separated the Trojans as he moved through the swirling dust, longing to kill Hector. He forgot the words of Achilles. Instead of turning back, he raced on to Troy.

He tried to reach the great walls three times, hurling himself among the Trojans as Hector watched from the gate. Then Patroclus charged a fourth time. He did not see Apollo behind him, wrapped in a cloak of mist. Apollo knocked off his helmet. And as Achilles' helmet rolled in the blood and dust for the first time, the Trojans saw that he was not Achilles.

As the dazed Patroclus stood there, a young Trojan speared him in the back. Patroclus pulled out the spear and retreated. But Hector ran after him, stabbing his enemy through the lower belly.

'Patroclus!' Hector shouted. 'The vultures will eat you on this spot! Even great Achilles could not save you.'

Patroclus, with his dying breath, replied, 'Zeus and Apollo gave you the victory. They conquered me, not you. You too have not long to live. You stand already in the shadow of death, by Achilles' hand.' As he spoke, death took him.

Hector put his foot on Patroclus' body, withdrew his bronze spear and left. Menelaus saw that Patroclus had been brought down. He advanced through the ranks and stood over his body, like a mother cow protecting her calf. Many Trojans came to taunt him and try to claim the body, and he killed one of their great leaders.

'What shall I do?' Menelaus asked himself. 'I cannot desert Patroclus who fell fighting for us. I shall find Ajax to help me. Although Hector will take the armour, we must try to bring the body back to Achilles.'

As soon as Menelaus had gone, Hector started to strip the body of its fine armour. But when he saw Ajax advancing with his great shield, he retreated to his chariot.

Now Ajax guarded Patroclus' body with his shield, like a lioness guards her cubs.

A fresh desire for battle filled Hector as he put on the shining armour of Achilles. He roused his men to fight with piercing shouts. The ground outside the walls of Troy was soaked with crimson blood, and Trojan bodies mingled with Greek bodies. The grim battle lasted all day, the battle for the body of Patroclus.

At last, out on the plain, Athene came to the rescue of the Greeks. Like a shimmering rainbow, she wrapped herself in a mist and plunged herself among the Greek armies, urging them on.

Achilles did not know what had happened. The battle was raging so far away, under the walls of Troy. He did not even think that Patroclus would try to enter Troy without him. Menelaus sent messengers to Achilles, to tell him of his friend's death.

'But even if Achilles wants to fight,' Menelaus thought, 'he cannot come to help us without his armour.'

As Patroclus' body was lifted from the ground, the Trojans chased the Greeks like hounds hunting a wounded animal. Hector and Aeneas pressed forward, and the Greek soldiers fled in front of them. But when the Greeks made a stand, they retreated. And in this way, the Greeks brought Patroclus' body back to the ships, through the battle that raged all round them like a fire.

CHAPTER EIGHT

A Change of Heart

When Achilles heard the news of his dear friend's death, a black cloud of grief engulfed him. He threw himself to the ground, smearing dust across his face and body. He pulled out handfuls of hair.

'O, Mother!' he cried. 'Patroclus is dead! I loved him as much as I love my own life. Hector has killed him and stripped him of my splendid armour. Hector shall pay for the blood of Patroclus. He shall die by my spear.'

'Then *you* do not have long to live,' his mother Thetis said. 'You are doomed to die immediately after Hector.'

'Then let me die!' Achilles cried.

'Do not forget that your armour is in Trojan hands, child,' his mother reminded him. 'Wait until tomorrow. I shall bring splendid new armour for you.'

While she made her way to Olympus, Hector caught up once more with Patroclus' body. Three times he caught hold of it, and three times Ajax beat him back. He would have taken the body if Achilles had not shown himself.

He stood on the highest wall, his body blazing with light against the sunset.

Three times his voice rang out. Three times the men of Troy were filled with fear. Three times their horses swerved away from the ditch. And as he shouted his fury, the Greeks pulled Patroclus from the Trojans.

Now the sun was setting and both sides withdrew. The Trojans, shocked by Achilles' return, could not rest.

'We should retreat to Troy,' Polydamas said. 'The Greeks were easy to deal with as long as Achilles had quarrelled with Agamemnon. But now I am terrified of swift-footed Achilles! He will never stay on the plain. He will come right into the heart of Troy.'

Hector flashed him an angry look. 'You ignorant fool!' he said. 'Do not put such cowardly ideas into our men. I shall not run away from Achilles. If he wants a fight, then he will have a fight. I shall meet him face to face.'

The Trojans shouted in agreement.

All through that night, they mourned for Patroclus in the Greek camps. In Olympus, the blacksmith built his great fires and forged fine armour for Achilles, a golden-crested helmet, and a shield decorated with battle pictures and a lion hunt. When dawn came, Thetis delivered the armour to her son. He was still weeping, his arms around Patroclus.

'Agamemnon and I must make peace,' Achilles said. 'Then I shall summon my men to battle.'

And so the quarrel ended.

The Greek soldiers shouted for joy. After making sacrifices to the gods, Achilles put on his armour. His eyes blazed like flames of fire, although grief still filled his heart. Then he raised the battle cry and, knowing that his own death was close, drove his powerful horses forward.

The Trojans lined up on the high ground of the plain. They shook in terror at the sight of Achilles. Athene thundered orders to the Greeks and Ares screamed like a squall of wind at the Trojans. And so the gods, encouraging both armies, set them at each other's throats. As the gods thundered, the earth trembled. Achilles went into battle, wild to fight Hector. But Apollo sent him only Aeneas.

The two champions faced each other, determined to do battle.

CHAPTER NINE

Revenge!

Aeneas was the first to step forward, brandishing his spear. Then Achilles sprang like a lion.

'Aeneas!' he shouted. 'Why have you stepped from the ranks to meet me? Are you hoping to step into old Priam's shoes when he dies? Have you forgotten that he has sons of his own? I suggest that you retreat now.'

'You cannot frighten me as you would a child,' Aeneas replied. 'I have heard enough of your words. Let us taste each other's spears!'

They fought hard. And it was only with the help of Poseidon that Aeneas escaped death.

'He has saved his skin this time,' Achilles thought, 'but he will not be anxious to face me again.' He leapt back into the ranks and shouted, 'Do not stand there waiting for the Trojans. Pick out your man and put your heart into the fight.'

Hector heard his words and shouted to his men, 'Proud Trojans, do not be frightened by Achilles. He is full of boasting words. I am going to fight him.'

The battle-cry went up. As Achilles sought out Hector, he fought like a madman with his spear, stabbing and chopping. With blood-curdling cries, he pushed through the Trojan ranks. His horses trampled men. The wheels of his chariot were sprayed with blood. The earth ran red as he pressed on, in search of glory and thirsty for revenge.

When the Greeks reached the River Scamander, Achilles

cut the Trojan army in two. One half he drove across the plain, towards Troy. The other half he herded into the river. The water whirled around them, echoing their cries. Achilles left his spear propped up against a tree and leaped into the water. With his sword, he hacked men to the right and to the left. The water turned red with their blood. When his arms were tired, he took twelve Trojans alive and sent them for slaughter down by the ships.

The Trojans ran like frightened fawns and took refuge in Troy. As the Greeks advanced, their shields together, Hector waited at the gate, clad in Achilles' old armour. But Achilles was furious that so many Trojans had managed to reach safety.

He cursed Apollo as he raced like a horse towards the walls of Troy. 'You have robbed me of a great victory,' he shouted.

King Priam was the first to see Achilles, shining like a star as he sped across the plain. The bronze of his armour gleamed. The old king groaned. 'Achilles has already robbed me of so many sons,' he wept to Hector. 'Do not fight him alone, my son. He is far stronger than you.'

But Hector stood firm at the gate, like a mountain snake waiting for a man beside its hole. Achilles came to him, his bronze armour glowing like a great fire. Hector trembled. Then he fled in terror. Achilles followed him like a mountain hawk. Three times they ran around the city walls. Achilles could not catch up with Hector and Hector could not shake off Achilles.

In Olympus, Zeus made up his mind. 'Athene shall decide whether Hector lives or dies,' he thought.

When they came again to the gate, Athene spoke to Achilles. 'Hector is hungry for battle, but you and I are going to kill him. I shall disguise myself as Hector's brother and bring him to you.'

And in this way, she led Hector forward.

'Achilles!' Hector said. 'I am not going to run from you any more. If Zeus allows it, I shall kill you and strip you of your armour.'

'There can be no pact between us,' Achilles replied, 'any more than there can be between a lion and a lamb. There is no way out. One of us must die.'

Hector shouted for his brother to bring him his long spear. But he was not there.

'So Athene has tricked me,' he said to himself. 'Evil death is now staring me in the face.'

With these words, Hector drew his sword and swooped on Achilles like a high-flying eagle diving on its prey. Achilles sprang to meet him, his heart full of savage hate, stabbing him on the neck where breastplate and helmet do not meet.

Hector sank to his knees, dying. 'Do not throw my body to the dogs,' he begged. 'Let my body be taken home for burial.'

But Achilles taunted him as he died. Then he did a shameful thing. He fastened Hector by the ankles to his chariot and rode towards the ships, dragging his body across the dusty, bloodstained ground.

Patroclus was buried according to custom, with funeral games and feasting. But Achilles was so full of grief that he took out his chariot in the night and dragged Hector's body round and round the camp. For twelve days he did this – until King Priam paid a heavy ransom for the body of his beloved son.

And there was a truce as they performed the funeral rites for the great Hector.

The Iliad *ends here. But the war went on: Achilles and Paris both died in battle. Even then, Helen was not returned to the Greeks.*

Virgil, a Roman writer, tells us how the Trojan War finally came to an end.

CHAPTER TEN

The Wooden Horse

The Greeks grew tired of the war. They wanted to sail home to see their wives and children. They attacked the walls of Troy many times, but the Trojans drove them back to their ships.

King Agamemnon called a council of leaders. 'How can we get inside Troy?' he asked Calchas.

'If strength has failed, we must use our cunning,' the priest replied.

Odysseus rose to his feet, for Athene had planted an idea in his mind. 'What if we built an enormous wooden horse?' he began. 'It would be hollow inside, and big enough for fifty men to hide there, including the bravest of our leaders. The armies will set sail for home, but the ships will hide by a far-off island, ready to sail back under cover of darkness.' Odysseus smiled. 'Now this is the cunning part. We shall leave one of our own men behind – a man whom the Trojans will not recognise. He will explain to the Trojans that the horse is a gift to Athene, to beg her not to send storms on the way home.'

Agamemnon approved of this plan. And a young Greek called Sinon volunteered to stay behind. Men were sent at once to chop down trees on the mountain sides. In only three days, the carpenters constructed the gigantic horse, taller than anything inside the Greek camp. Fifty men climbed inside, including Odysseus, Menelaus and Diomedes. They wore soft cloaks around their bodies, to muffle the sound of their clanking armour. Now, at last, Agamemnon prepared the ships to sail.

From the walls of Troy, the Trojans saw the burning of the Greek camps and the ships setting out to sea. And when they caught sight of that great gleaming horse standing on the plain, they wondered why it had been left there. They unfastened their gates, tired of being trapped for so long. Like swarming bees, they thronged to the deserted Greek camps.

One of the Trojan priests, Laocoon, tried to stop them. 'Has madness overtaken your brains?' he asked. 'You know how cunning Odysseus is. Do you *really* believe the Greeks have gone? How do we know our enemies are not inside this horse? Do not trust them. And do not bring it back to Troy.' He hurled his spear at the horse and heard a hollow sound.

Laocoon might have gone closer. But, at that moment, men brought forward Sinon, whom they had found hiding near the river.

'Alas!' Sinon wept, trembling. 'I wish that I were dead! My fellow Greeks have accused me of crimes I did not commit. They would have killed me if I hadn't escaped.'

'Why have they left this wooden horse?' the Trojans asked.

'It's a peace offering for Athene,' Sinon replied. 'If you destroy it, Troy will burn to the ground. Take it into the city and you will be glorious.'

The Trojans, moved by his tears and his words, untied him. 'Forget the Greeks,' they said, 'and stay with us.'

And by fawning words, he did what ten years of fighting had not – he won over the Trojans.

But a dreadful thing happened. The sea divided at that moment, and from it rose two serpents, their forked tongues winding around Laocoon's sons, and around Laocoon himself. Then they disappeared, leaving their mangled bodies on the seashore.

King Priam watched in horror. 'Athene is angry because we threw a spear at her gift,' he said. 'We must anger her no more. Fix wooden rollers beneath the horse!' he commanded. 'And bring ropes! We must take the horse to Troy at once.'

The Trojans hauled the horse along the steep streets of Troy and placed it inside the temple of Athene. And the people feasted and danced until night fell. As they slept, Sinon – standing on the temple wall – watched for the lights of the Greek ships returning. At last, he saw them.

Sinon ran to the wooden horse and called for the trapdoor to be opened up. One by one, the Greek men slid on ropes to the ground. Then they went straight to the gates of Troy and killed the guards. Now Troy was open for the Greek army. The soldiers poured through the gates like a river of flame.

Trumpets sounded the alarm. Trojans rushed to defend the walls. But it was too late! Clashing spears and terrified cries pierced the night air. The slaughter that night was terrible to watch. Even women and children were hacked to pieces. Houses and temples floated in blood. King Priam was slain as he knelt to pray, and his wives and daughters taken into captivity. Nothing could hold the Greek soldiers back.

Death came, whether by fighting or by fleeing.

As Troy burned, Helen hid in the house of Paris' brother, fearing a Trojan sword in revenge for Priam's death – and dreading the revenge of the husband she had deserted. Here Menelaus found her. But Odysseus was standing in the doorway.

'I beg for the life of the beautiful Helen,' he said.

Helen's life was spared. Love replaced the anger that Menelaus had so long felt for her. And Helen, who had been the cause of that terrible fighting, went back to her husband's ship as his queen.

The Greek ships set sail at last. The long war was over – and Troy, its temples and the great horse had been consumed by fire.